Berenice

A Dark Exploration of Obsession, Death & the Unsettling Fragility of Beauty

A Modern Translation
Adapted for the Contemporary Reader

Edgar Allan Poe

Translated by Tim Zengerink

Table Of Contents

Preface
Message to the Reader

Rebuilding the Greatest Library in Human History

Thousands of years ago, the Library of Alexandria was the heart of global knowledge — a sanctuary where the wisdom of every known civilization was gathered and shared freely.

And then, it was lost.

Now, we're rebuilding it — and you are invited to join us.

At the Library of Alexandria, we've set out to make every book available to every person on Earth — not just in print, but in every language, every format, and for every reader.

Here's how we do it:

- **Deluxe Print Editions at True Printing Cost** - Order any book as a high-quality paperback, elegant hardcover, or stunning boxset — and only pay what it costs to print. No markups. No middlemen.
- **Unlimited Access to the Greatest Works** - Enjoy thousands of timeless classics — from Plato to Shakespeare to Tolstoy — in beautiful, modern eBook and audiobook editions. Read and listen without limits — for every reader, everywhere.
- **Modern Translations for Every Language & Dialect** - We're reimagining the classics in clear, accessible language — and translating them into every dialect imaginable. Everyone deserves to understand humanity's greatest ideas.

When you visit **LibraryofAlexandria.com**, you're not just accessing books — you're joining a global movement to restore, preserve, and share the wisdom of civilization.

Join us today at LibraryofAlexandria.com

Together, we'll ensure the light of human wisdom never fades again.

With gratitude,

The Modern Library of Alexandria Team

Visit:
www.libraryofalexandria.com
Or scan the code below:

Introduction

The Shadowed Mind of Poe and the Birth of Gothic Terror

Among the many unsettling masterpieces of Edgar Allan Poe, Berenice stands out as a work that explores the darker recesses of the human mind, the horrors of physical decay, and the obsessive impulses that lurk beneath the surface of sanity. First published in *The Southern Literary Messenger* in March 1835, this short story is an early yet remarkably potent example of Poe's signature blend of psychological horror, morbidity, and poetic intensity. It is a tale that not only unnerves but also provokes reflection on the fragility of beauty, the inevitability of death, and the thin line that separates rational thought from destructive obsession.

The story is narrated by Egaeus, a man plagued by a peculiar mental disorder that compels him to fixate obsessively on specific objects. His cousin Berenice, once a vibrant and beautiful woman, falls ill and undergoes a terrifying physical transformation. Her vitality drains away, leaving her emaciated and near death. Yet, instead of pity or fear, Egaeus becomes consumed by a single aspect of her deteriorating form: her teeth. These teeth, white and perfect amidst the decay of her body, become the focus of his monomania—a psychological fixation so intense that it leads him to commit a grotesque act. When Berenice is mistakenly buried alive, Egaeus, in a state of fevered obsession, exhumes her body and removes her teeth. The story closes with this horrifying revelation, leaving readers unsettled by the depths of Egaeus's madness.

In this single, brief narrative, Poe encapsulates many of the themes and techniques that define his body of work. He blends Gothic horror with psychological realism, creating a narrative that is as much about the inner torment of the protagonist as it is about external events. *Berenice* is not simply a tale of death and decay; it is an exploration of how obsession can distort reality, consuming both the mind and the soul. The story's power lies in its ability to evoke visceral fear while also engaging the intellect, inviting readers to consider the nature of beauty, mortality, and mental illness.

To fully appreciate *Berenice*, it is important to understand its historical and literary context. In the early 19th century, American literature was still finding its voice, and Poe was one of the first writers to elevate the short story to an art form. His works, often published in magazines and literary journals, were notable for their psychological depth, meticulous structure, and ability to evoke intense emotion. *Berenice*, with its unsettling focus on decay and monomania, shocked some contemporary readers, leading Poe to revise certain passages in later editions to tone down the story's graphic elements. Yet even in its softened form, the story remains one of the most disturbing explorations of morbid fascination in American literature.

At the time Poe wrote *Berenice*, Gothic fiction was already well established, with writers like Mary Shelley, Ann Radcliffe, and Charles Maturin shaping the genre. However, Poe brought something uniquely personal to Gothic literature. His stories are not set in far-off castles or populated by stock villains; instead, they delve into the labyrinth of the human psyche, turning the mind itself into a haunted house. In *Berenice*, the horror does not arise from supernatural forces but from the obsessive focus of Egaeus, whose mental illness drives him to commit acts of unspeakable cruelty.

This focus on psychological terror rather than external monsters was revolutionary. Poe understood that the most terrifying experiences are often internal—the result of fractured thoughts, uncontrollable compulsions, and the slow erosion of reason. *Berenice* demonstrates this insight with chilling clarity, portraying a protagonist whose mind is both the stage and the architect of horror. For modern readers, this psychological dimension makes the story not only frightening but also hauntingly relatable, as it forces us to confront the darker impulses that may reside within us all.

Obsession, Decay, and the Fragility of Beauty

One of the most striking themes of *Berenice* is the destructive power of obsession. Egaeus's monomania—a compulsive focus on one idea or object—serves as the driving force of the narrative. Poe was fascinated by mental disorders and the ways they could distort perception and behavior, and Egaeus is one of his earliest and most vivid portrayals of a mind consumed by a single, overpowering fixation. His obsession with Berenice's teeth is both grotesque and symbolic. The teeth, perfect and uncorrupted amidst the decay of her body, represent an enduring fragment of beauty in a world otherwise dominated by decline and death. Yet, by fixating on this detail, Egaeus reduces Berenice from a living person to an object of morbid fascination, stripping her of humanity.

This reduction of a person to a mere collection of parts is one of the story's most disturbing elements. Poe invites readers to consider the ways in which beauty can be both cherished and corrupted by the human mind. In Egaeus's gaze, Berenice's beauty becomes a source of torment rather than admiration. As her illness progresses, her body deteriorates, and Egaeus, rather than feeling compassion, becomes increasingly fixated on the one part of her that remains untouched by decay. This obsessive focus leads to a chilling act of violence that underscores the danger of allowing beauty to become an idol divorced from humanity.

The theme of decay is central to *Berenice*. From the opening paragraphs, Poe sets a tone of morbidity, describing the decline of both Berenice's health and Egaeus's mental state. The story is filled with imagery of death, disease, and rot, creating an atmosphere that is both oppressive and hypnotic. Poe's fascination with death—its inevitability, its physical realities, and its psychological impact—permeates the narrative. Berenice's illness and premature burial are not simply plot devices; they are manifestations of the story's broader meditation on the transient nature of beauty and life.

Poe's exploration of beauty in *Berenice* is particularly noteworthy. Unlike the idealized beauty often celebrated in literature, Berenice's beauty is fragile, fleeting, and ultimately horrifying. As her illness consumes her, her once-vivid features become distorted, and Egaeus's fixation on her teeth becomes a grotesque reminder of the impermanence of physical perfection. In this way, the story serves as a dark counterpoint to traditional romantic notions of beauty, suggesting that our attempts to preserve or possess beauty can lead to madness and destruction.

Another layer of meaning in *Berenice* lies in its portrayal of mental illness. Egaeus's condition is described with unsettling precision, reflecting Poe's interest in the workings of the human mind. His monomania, with its repetitive thoughts and compulsive behaviors, anticipates modern understandings of obsessive-compulsive disorders. By presenting the story through Egaeus's first-person perspective, Poe immerses the reader in the protagonist's distorted worldview, making us complicit in his descent into madness. This narrative technique not only heightens the horror but also invites empathy, as we glimpse the torment of a mind at war with itself.

The story's climax—the exhumation and mutilation of Berenice—is one of the most shocking moments in Poe's oeuvre. Though the act itself is not described in explicit detail (particularly in the revised versions), the implication is clear, and its psychological impact is profound. Egaeus's realization of what he has done, conveyed through the discovery of the blood-stained dental instruments, is both horrifying and tragic. It is the culmination of a narrative that has meticulously built an atmosphere of dread, leading to a conclusion that is as inevitable as it is disturbing.

Poe's Craft, Legacy, and the Reader's Experience

To fully appreciate *Berenice*, one must consider Poe's craftsmanship as a writer. His mastery of language, tone, and structure is evident in every sentence. The story begins with a philosophical meditation on life, death, and the nature of the mind, drawing the reader into a reflective and somber mood. As the narrative progresses, Poe carefully layers imagery and symbolism, creating a sense of unease that grows with each page. The pacing is deliberate, mirroring Egaeus's obsessive focus and leading the reader inexorably toward the story's horrific climax.

Poe's use of first-person narration is particularly effective in *Berenice*. By filtering the story through Egaeus's consciousness, Poe blurs the line between reality and delusion, forcing readers to experience the world as the protagonist does—fragmented, distorted, and consumed by fixation. This narrative choice not only enhances the psychological depth of the story but also aligns with Poe's broader interest in unreliable narrators, a device he employed in many of his most famous works, including *The Tell-Tale Heart* and *The Black Cat*.

The legacy of Berenice is significant. Though it is not as widely known as some of Poe's other tales, it remains a key work in his exploration of psychological horror. Its themes of obsession, decay, and the fragility of beauty have influenced countless writers, filmmakers, and artists. The story's focus on mental illness and the darker aspects of human psychology also anticipates the development of modern horror, which often draws on psychological realism to create fear.

For the reader, *Berenice* offers a complex and unsettling experience. It is not a story that provides easy answers or comforting resolutions. Instead, it challenges us to confront uncomfortable truths about the human condition: our fascination with beauty, our fear of death, and the destructive power of obsession. By immersing us in the mind of Egaeus, Poe forces us to grapple with the possibility that madness is not an external force but an aspect of our own humanity.

As you prepare to read *Berenice*, it is worth approaching the story not only as a work of horror but also as a work of psychological and philosophical inquiry. Pay attention to Poe's language, which is rich with metaphor and rhythm, creating a hypnotic effect that mirrors the obsessive thoughts of the narrator. Notice how Poe uses imagery of light and darkness, life and death, beauty and decay, to build a world that is both haunting and eerily familiar. And consider the ways in which the story resonates with contemporary concerns about mental health, identity, and the fleeting nature of physical perfection.

In conclusion, *Berenice* is a story that lingers long after the final sentence. Its power lies not only in its shocking climax but in its ability to evoke a deep, unsettling awareness of the fragility of life and the dangerous allure of obsession. It is a work that embodies Poe's genius for blending the poetic with the macabre, the psychological with the philosophical. As you delve into its pages, prepare to enter a world where beauty is both a blessing and a curse, where the mind can become its own worst enemy, and where the line between admiration and destruction is perilously thin.

Berenice

Misery comes in many forms. The suffering of our world takes countless shapes. Stretching across the vast horizon like a rainbow, its colors are as varied as those of that arc—each one distinct, yet seamlessly woven together. Stretching across the vast horizon like a rainbow! How is it that I have drawn an image of ugliness from something beautiful?—taken a symbol of sorrow from a promise of peace? But just as, in moral philosophy, evil emerges from good, so in reality, sorrow is born from joy. Either the memory of past happiness becomes today's pain, or the suffering we experience now stems from the bliss that could have been.

My baptismal name is Egaeus; I will not reveal my family name. However, there are no towers in the land more ancient and respected than my dark, gray, ancestral halls. Our lineage has been known as a family of dreamers and visionaries; and in many remarkable details—in the character of the family estate—in the frescoes of the main hall—in the tapestries of the bedrooms—in the carved stonework of some supports in the armory—but most notably in the gallery of ancient paintings—in the design of the library room—and, finally, in the very unusual nature of the library's collection—there is more than enough evidence to support this belief.

My earliest memories are tied to that room and its books—though I won't say more about those volumes. My mother died there. I was born in that same place. But it's pointless to claim I hadn't lived before—that the soul doesn't have a prior existence. Do you disagree? Let's not debate it. I'm convinced of it myself, but I'm not trying to convince anyone else. There is, though, a memory of ethereal shapes—of spiritual and meaningful eyes—of sounds that were musical yet melancholy—a memory that refuses to be pushed away; a recollection like a shadow—unclear, shifting, vague, unstable; and like a shadow too in how impossible it is for me to escape it as long as the light of my reasoning mind continues to exist.

I was born in that room. Awakening from what felt like a long night of nonexistence—though it wasn't truly that—I found myself suddenly transported into the realm of fairy tales, into a palace built from imagination, into the untamed territories of scholarly contemplation and learning. It's not surprising that I looked around with shocked and passionate eyes, that I spent my childhood lost in books and wasted my youth lost in daydreams. What is surprising is that as the years passed and I reached the height of manhood while still living in my family's house, a remarkable stagnation settled over the vital forces of my life. It's amazing how completely my ordinary thoughts transformed in character. The real world began to affect me only as illusions and nothing more, while the fantastic ideas from the realm of dreams became not just the substance of my daily life, but actually became that life entirely and exclusively.

Berenice and I were cousins, and we grew up together in my father's house. But we developed very differently—I was sickly and consumed by darkness, while she was nimble, graceful, and bursting with vitality. She loved wandering the hillsides, while I preferred scholarly pursuits in quiet seclusion. I lived inside my own mind, completely devoted in body and soul to the most intense and agonizing contemplation, while she moved through life without a care, never thinking about the shadows that crossed her path or the silent passage of time's dark wings. Berenice! I call out her name—Berenice! And from the gray wreckage of memory, a thousand chaotic memories are awakened by that sound! How clearly I can see her now, just as she was in those early days of carefree happiness and joy! What magnificent yet otherworldly beauty! Like a spirit among the gardens of Arnheim! Like a water nymph beside its fountains! And then—then everything becomes mystery and horror, a story that shouldn't be told. Disease—a deadly disease—struck her body like a desert wind, and even as I watched her, the force of transformation swept through her, affecting her mind, her behavior, and her personality, and in the most subtle and terrifying way, even changing her very identity! The destroyer came and left, and where is the victim now? I didn't recognize her—or no longer knew her as Berenice.

Among the many illnesses that followed that devastating primary condition which brought about such a terrible transformation in my cousin's moral and physical state, the most distressing and persistent was a form of epilepsy that often ended in a trance-like state—a trance that closely resembled actual death, and from which she would recover in most cases with startling suddenness. Meanwhile, my own illness—for I have been told I should call it nothing else—my own illness grew rapidly worse and eventually took on the characteristics of an unusual and extraordinary type of obsession that gained strength by the hour and minute, ultimately gaining an incomprehensible hold over me. This obsession, if I must call it that, involved a diseased oversensitivity of those mental faculties that metaphysical science calls attention. I probably won't be understood, but I'm afraid it's impossible to give the average reader an adequate sense of the nervous intensity of interest with which my powers of deep thought became completely absorbed in contemplating even the most common objects in the world.

To spend long, tireless hours lost in thought, with my focus completely captured by some trivial detail in the margin or in the printed text of a book; to become completely engrossed, for most of a summer day, in an unusual shadow cast diagonally across the tapestry or the floor; to lose myself for an entire night watching the constant flame of a lamp or the glowing coals of a fire; to spend whole days daydreaming over the scent of a flower; to repeat endlessly some ordinary word until the sound, through constant repetition, no longer carried any meaning to the mind; to lose all awareness of movement or physical being through complete bodily stillness maintained stubbornly for long periods: these were some of the most frequent and least harmful peculiarities brought on by a state of mental functioning that was not entirely without precedent, but certainly resisted any attempt at analysis or explanation.

Yet let me not be misunderstood. The excessive, intense, and unhealthy attention that trivial objects aroused in this way must not be confused with that reflective tendency common to all people, and especially indulged in by those with vivid imaginations. It was not even, as might be initially assumed, an extreme condition or exaggeration of such a tendency, but fundamentally and essentially distinct and different. In one case, the dreamer or enthusiast, being interested by an object that is usually not trivial, gradually loses sight of this object in a maze of deductions and suggestions arising from it, until, at the end of a daydream often filled with pleasure, he finds the starting point, or first cause of his thoughts, completely vanished and forgotten. In my case, the primary object was always trivial, although it took on, through my disturbed perception, a distorted and unreal importance. Few deductions, if any, were made; and those few stubbornly returned to the original object as a center. The meditations were never pleasurable; and, at the end of the reverie, the first cause, far from being out of sight, had gained that unnaturally exaggerated interest which was the dominant characteristic of the disease. In short, the mental powers most particularly exercised were, with me, as I have said before, the attentive, and are, with the day-dreamer, the speculative.

My books during this time, while they may not have directly worsened my condition, clearly shared many of the same imaginative and disconnected qualities that characterized the disorder itself. I clearly recall, among others, the treatise by the distinguished Italian scholar Coelius Secundus Curio, "De Amplitudine Beati Regni Dei;" St. Augustine's masterwork, the "City of God;" and Tertullian's "De Carne Christi," in which the paradoxical statement "Mortuus est Dei filius; credible est quia ineptum est: et sepultus resurrexit; certum est quia impossibile est" consumed all of my attention for many weeks of intense and unproductive study.

Thus it became clear that, disturbed from its equilibrium only by minor matters, my reasoning resembled that ocean cliff described by Ptolemy Hephestion, which consistently withstood the assaults of human force and the more savage rage of waters and winds, yet trembled only at the touch of the flower known as Asphodel. And while, to a superficial observer, it might seem certain that the transformation caused by her tragic illness in Berenice's moral state would provide me with numerous subjects for that intense and unusual contemplation whose character I have taken considerable effort to describe, this was not at all the situation. During the clear periods of my affliction, her misfortune did indeed cause me anguish, and deeply feeling the complete destruction of her beautiful and kind existence, I regularly engaged in frequent and painful consideration of the miraculous methods by which such an extraordinary change had been so suddenly accomplished. However, these thoughts did not share the peculiar nature of my condition and were the kind that would have emerged, under comparable circumstances, in ordinary people. Faithful to its distinctive nature, my disorder delighted in the less significant but more shocking alterations created in Berenice's physical form—in the remarkable and most horrifying transformation of her personal identity.

During the peak of her extraordinary beauty, I certainly had never loved her. In the peculiar contradiction of my existence, my emotions had never originated from the heart, and my desires always stemmed from the mind. Through the gray light of early morning—among the latticed shadows of the forest at midday—and in the quiet of my library at night—she had passed before my eyes, and I had observed her—not as the living and breathing Berenice, but as the Berenice of a dream; not as a creature of the earth, earthly, but as the concept of such a creature; not as something to admire, but to examine; not as an object of love, but as the subject of the most complex yet scattered contemplation. And now—now I trembled in her presence, and turned pale at her approach; yet, bitterly mourning her fallen and wretched state, I remembered that she had loved me for a long time, and, in a moment of poor judgment, I spoke to her of marriage.

And eventually the time of our wedding was drawing near, when one afternoon in the winter of that year—one of those unusually warm, calm, and foggy days that nurture the beautiful Halcyon (*1)—I sat (and sat, as I believed, alone) in the inner room of the library. But when I raised my eyes, I saw that Berenice was standing before me.

Was it my overactive imagination—or the hazy effect of the air—or the dim twilight in the room—or the gray curtains that draped around her form—that made her outline seem so wavering and unclear? I couldn't say. She didn't speak a word; and I—nothing in the world could have made me utter a sound. A freezing chill shot through my body; a feeling of unbearable dread weighed down on me; an overwhelming curiosity filled my entire being; and falling back into the chair, I sat there for some time unable to breathe or move, my eyes locked on her figure. Unfortunately! her wasting away was extreme, and not a single trace of who she used to be remained in any part of her shape. My intense stare finally moved to her face.

The forehead was high and very pale, with an unusual calmness to it; the once jet-black hair fell partly across it, casting shadows over the sunken temples with countless curls that were now a bright yellow, clashing harshly in their strange appearance with the deep sadness that dominated the face. The eyes were lifeless and dull, appearing to have no pupils at all, and I instinctively pulled back from their glassy stare to focus instead on the thin and withered lips. They opened; and with a smile that held a strange significance, the teeth of the transformed Berenice slowly revealed themselves to me. I wish to God that I had never seen them, or that after seeing them, I had died!

The sound of a door closing startled me, and when I looked up, I discovered that my cousin had left the room. But from the chaotic chambers of my mind, the white and ghostly image of those teeth had not departed—and would not be driven away. Not a single mark on their surface—not a hint of discoloration on their enamel—not a single indentation along their edges—everything about that moment when she smiled had been burned into my memory. I could see them now even more clearly than when I had actually looked at them. The teeth!—the teeth!—they were here, there, and everywhere, visible and tangible before me; long, narrow, and extremely white, with those pale lips twisting around them, just as they had in that first terrible moment when I noticed them. Then the complete madness of my obsession took hold, and I fought uselessly against its strange and overwhelming power. Among all the countless things in the world around me, I could think of nothing but those teeth. I craved them with a frenzied longing. Everything else and all other concerns were swallowed up by my single-minded focus on them. They—and only they—filled my mind's eye, and they alone became the center of my entire mental existence. I examined them from every angle. I rotated them in every position. I studied their features. I focused on their unique qualities. I contemplated their structure. I reflected on how their nature might change. I trembled as I imagined them having feeling and awareness, and even without the lips, being capable of expressing emotion. About Mademoiselle Salle it has been rightly said, "Que tous ses pas etaient des sentiments," and about Berenice I believed even more seriously que toutes ses dents etaient des idées. Des idées!—ah, there was the insane thought that ruined me! Des idées!—ah, that was why I desired them so desperately! I believed that possessing them was the only way I could find peace again, the only way to restore my sanity.

And the evening closed in around me like this—and then darkness came, stayed for a while, and left—and day broke again—and the mists of a second night were now gathering—and still I sat motionless in that lonely room— and still I sat lost in deep thought—and still the ghostly vision of the teeth held its terrible power over me, floating with the most vivid and hideous clarity among the shifting lights and shadows of the room. Finally, a cry of horror and alarm broke through my thoughts; and after a moment of silence, this was followed by the sound of distressed voices, mixed with many quiet moans of grief or pain. I got up from my chair, and opening one of the library doors, I saw standing in the outer room a servant girl, crying, who told me that Berenice was—dead! She had suffered an epileptic seizure early that morning, and now, as night was falling, the grave was prepared for its occupant, and all the arrangements for the burial were complete.

I found myself sitting in the library, once again sitting there alone. It felt as though I had just awakened from a confusing and disturbing dream. I knew it was now midnight, and I was fully aware that since the sun had set, Berenice had been buried. But of that grim period in between, I had no clear, or at least no definite understanding. Yet the memory was filled with horror—horror made more horrible by being unclear, and terror made more terrible by its uncertainty. It was a frightening page in the record of my existence, covered entirely with dim, hideous, and incomprehensible memories. I struggled to decode them, but without success; while again and again, like the ghost of a vanished sound, the sharp and piercing scream of a woman's voice seemed to echo in my ears. I had committed an act—what was it? I asked myself the question out loud, and the whispering echoes of the room answered me,—"What was it?"

A lamp flickered on the table next to me, and beside it sat a small box. There was nothing particularly special about it, and I had seen it many times before, since it belonged to our family doctor. But what was it doing there on my table, and why did I tremble when I looked at it? I couldn't explain any of this, and eventually my gaze fell to the open pages of a book and to a sentence that had been underlined. The words were the unusual yet simple ones from the poet Ebn Zaiat: "Dicebant mihi sodales si sepulchrum amicae visitarem, curas meas aliquantulum fore levatas." So why, as I read them, did the hair on my head stand on end, and why did the blood in my body freeze in my veins?

A soft knock came at the library door, and a servant entered on tiptoe, as pale as someone from a grave. His expression was wild with terror, and he spoke to me in a voice that shook, was hoarse, and very quiet. What did he say? I caught only fragments of his broken sentences. He spoke of a wild scream that had shattered the night's silence, of the household gathering together, of searching in the direction where the sound had come from. Then his voice became chillingly clear as he whispered to me about a desecrated grave, about a mangled body wrapped in burial cloth, yet still breathing, still with a beating heart, still alive!

He pointed to the clothing—it was dirty and covered with dried blood. I said nothing, and he gently took my hand: it bore the marks of human fingernails pressed into the skin. He drew my attention to something against the wall. I stared at it for several minutes: it was a shovel. With a scream I leaped to the table and grabbed the box that rested on top of it. But I couldn't pry it open; and in my shaking, it slipped from my grasp and fell hard, breaking into pieces; and from it, with a clattering noise, there spilled out some dental surgery tools, mixed with thirty-two small, white and ivory-colored objects that scattered across the floor.

THE END

Thank You For Reading

You've Just Read a Piece of the Greatest Library Ever Rebuilt

Thank you for reading.

This book is one of thousands we're restoring, reimagining, and translating as part of the **Modern Library of Alexandria** — a global movement to preserve and share humanity's most important ideas.

What was once lost to fire and time is now rising again — not just as memory, but as living, breathing knowledge, freely accessible to all.

What You Can Do Next:

- **Keep Reading.**

  Discover more legendary works — in beautiful print, audiobook, or digital form — at LibraryofAlexandria.com.

- **Build Your Own Library.**

  Every title is available as a paperback, hardcover, or collectible boxset — at true printing cost. Craft a personal library worthy of display.

- **Spread the Light.**

  Share this book. Tell others about the movement. Help us translate every timeless work into every language, so no reader is ever left behind.

By finishing this book, you've already taken part in something extraordinary.

Join us at LibraryofAlexandria.com

Together, we're rebuilding the greatest library the world has ever known.

With appreciation,

The Modern Library of Alexandria Team

Visit:
www.libraryofalexandria.com
Or scan the code below: